THE PRINCIPLES OF DEMOCRACY

WHAT IS COMPROMISE?

JOSHUA TURNER

PowerKiDS press

New York

Published in 2020 by The Rosen Publishing Group, Inc.
29 East 21st Street, New York, NY 10010

Copyright © 2020 by The Rosen Publishing Group, Inc.

All rights reserved. No part of this book may be reproduced in any form without permission in writing from the publisher, except by a reviewer.

First Edition

Editor: Melissa Raé Shofner
Book Design: Reann Nye

Photo Credits: Seriest art Bplanet/Shutterstock.com; cover gradyreese/E+/Getty Images; p. 5 BRENDAN SMIALOWSKI/AFP/Getty Images; p. 7 Thomas Barwick/Stone/Getty Images; p. 9 https://commons.wikimedia.org/wiki/File:Declaration_of_Independence_(1819),_by_John_Trumbull.jpg; p. 11 Orhan Cam/Shutterstock.com; p. 13 SOPA Images/LightRocket/Getty Images; p. 15 Stockbyte/Getty Images; p. 17 Tasos Katopodis/Getty Images News/Getty Images; p. 19 Dave and Les Jacobs/Blend Images/Getty Images; p. 21 gg-foto/Shutterstock.com; p. 22 Supawadee56/Shutterstock.com.

Cataloging-in-Publication Data

Names: Turner, Joshua.
Title: What is compromise? / Joshua Turner.
Description: New York : PowerKids Press, 2020. | Series: The principles of democracy | Includes glossary and index.
Identifiers: ISBN 9781538342640 (pbk.) | ISBN 9781538342664 (library bound) | ISBN 9781538342657 (6 pack)
Subjects: LCSH: Political ethics–Juvenile literature. | Interpersonal relations–Juvenile literature. | Compromise (Ethics).
Classification: LCC JA79.T87 2019 | DDC 172–dc23

Manufactured in the United States of America

CPSIA Compliance Information: Batch #CSPK19: For Further Information contact Rosen Publishing, New York, New York at 1-800-237-9932

CONTENTS

★★★★★★★★★★

WHAT IS COMPROMISE? 4
WHY IS COMPROMISE IMPORTANT? .. 6
COMPROMISE AND DEMOCRACY 8
MAKING LAWS 10
WHEN SHOULD
    YOU NOT COMPROMISE? 12
CAN COMPROMISE BE BAD? 14
EFFECTIVENESS VS. VALUES 16
WHAT KIND OF
    LEADERS DO YOU WANT? 18
DEMOCRACY AND
    THE GREATER GOOD 20
COMPROMISE IN EVERYDAY LIFE ... 22
GLOSSARY 23
INDEX 24
WEBSITES 24

WHAT IS COMPROMISE?

Imagine you and your friends are trying to decide what game to play. There are some games you love and some you dislike, but nobody can agree on a single game.

Instead of choosing a game that will make some people happy and some people upset, you should play a game that everyone likes at least a little bit. This is called compromise. When you compromise, nobody gets exactly what they want, but nobody is very unhappy either.

THE SPIRIT OF DEMOCRACY

The Ancient Greeks were among the first people to use compromise as a **foundation** for government. They had one of the first democracies in the world.

In 2016, President Barack Obama visited Greece, the birthplace of democracy and of compromise as a **principle** of government.

5

WHY IS COMPROMISE IMPORTANT?

Compromise is important because it allows society to **function** well. No one can get everything they want all the time. Without compromise, people would often be very unhappy.

Some people are better at compromising than others. These people are often happier. They're also nicer to be around. People who are good at compromising make other people happy, too. When people have trouble compromising, they often fight and argue instead of working out their problems.

Compromise is important in many areas of life. On sports teams, players need to compromise and work together to win games.

COMPROMISE AND DEMOCRACY

Democracy is a system of government in which everyone gets a say. This makes compromise very important. A democracy can't work well if people aren't willing to give something up in order to get something else.

This means people need to **communicate** what issues or problems they're willing to compromise on. They must also say what they won't give up no matter what. Honesty and a willingness to see others' points of view are key to compromise in a democracy.

THE SPIRIT OF DEMOCRACY

The Founding Fathers of the United States couldn't agree on everything, but through compromise they were able to found a country that has done well for over 200 years.

Setting up a new country is no easy task, especially when there are many people involved. The Founding Fathers were able to compromise on deeply held beliefs when founding the United States.

MAKING LAWS

★★★★★★★★★

The most important job of any government is to make laws. But how can a government make laws that millions of people will agree with? Again, the key is compromise. As long as the laws apply equally to all people, then compromise is easier to reach.

People may not like all the laws, but with compromise they'll see that some laws will be better for them than others. They'll also see that everyone has a fair chance in the end.

Lawmakers at our nation's capitol must compromise to make the laws we all live by.

WHEN SHOULD YOU NOT COMPROMISE?

Sometimes you may come across an issue or belief that you just don't feel comfortable compromising on, and that's OK. Compromise may make you a little uncomfortable at times because you have to see things from someone else's point of view.

There may be times when compromise can't be reached without you feeling quite uncomfortable. There's no way to tell when you shouldn't compromise. You should judge each **specific** case based on your own personal feelings.

THE SPIRIT OF DEMOCRACY

Abraham Lincoln was asked to compromise with Southern states over the issue of slavery at the end of the Civil War. But Lincoln couldn't compromise on this issue and instead passed the Thirteenth Amendment, which ended slavery.

At **rallies**, people express views they aren't willing to compromise on.

CAN COMPROMISE BE BAD?

As great and important as compromise may be, there are times when it can be bad. Imagine a friend wants you to break the rules while another friend does not. You all compromise to break the rules a little bit. This kind of compromise still means you're breaking the rules, and that's not good.

Compromise is bad when it still leads to people getting hurt or treated unfairly. These are decisions a person must make on a case-by-case basis.

> Before compromising, think about what you care about. If the end result will go against what's most important to you, it's probably not a good idea to make the compromise.

EFFECTIVENESS VS. VALUES

When deciding whether or not to compromise, you have to think about effectiveness and values. Effectiveness is the ability to get something done. Values are the things you care about.

Is getting something done more important to you than how you feel about a bad outcome? People have to think about this every day when making decisions. These kinds of decisions about values and effectiveness are what drive **debate** in our government. They're also what helps make democracy great.

THE SPIRIT OF DEMOCRACY

When passing his important health care law, Barack Obama was forced to compromise some parts of it. He felt that getting something passed that was good was better than getting nothing passed at all.

Politicians must decide whether compromise is better than doing little or nothing.

WHAT KIND OF LEADERS DO YOU WANT?

When thinking about compromise and democracy, you should think about what sort of leaders you want. Do you want leaders who are willing to work with people they disagree with, or do you want leaders who will fight for their own principles most of the time?

The answer to this question can tell you a lot about what kind of government you want to live under. It'll also tell you a bit about yourself and how you might **interact** with other people.

The ability of leaders to compromise will often help decide how a country feels about specific issues.

DEMOCRACY AND THE GREATER GOOD

When thinking about why people compromise in democracies, it's important to consider the greater good. Sometimes decisions may not make everyone happy, but they're done because they serve a greater good that may not always be easy to see.

In a democracy, you must think about how decisions **affect** everyone, not just yourself. Compromise allows everyone to get a little bit of what they want. This is usually better for everybody, which means it's for the greater good.

THE SPIRIT OF DEMOCRACY

Even as far back as ancient Rome, senators had to make decisions and compromises based on what was best for all citizens. This is a **tradition** that carries on today in democracies around the world.

Compromise for the greater good is a democratic principle that goes all the way back to Ancient Rome.

21

COMPROMISE IN EVERYDAY LIFE

★★★★★★★★★★

While compromise is important in any democracy, it's just as important in your everyday life. Knowing when to compromise and when to stand firm for your values is an important part of being a good citizen.

The more you learn and the more **experience** you have, the better you'll be at compromising and making good decisions. When it comes to compromise, you should keep in mind that you might not always get what you want, but you'll often get what you need.

GLOSSARY

affect: To act on someone or something and cause a change.

communicate: To share ideas and feelings through sounds and motions.

debate: A discussion in which people share different opinions about something.

experience: Skill or knowledge you get by doing something.

foundation: An idea or thought that provides support for something.

function: To work or operate.

interact: To come together and have an effect on each other.

principle: A moral rule or belief that helps you know right from wrong and that affects your actions.

rally: A public meeting to support or oppose someone or something.

specific: Special or particular.

tradition: A way of thinking, behaving, or doing something that's been used by people in a particular society for a long time.

INDEX

A
arguing, 6

C
citizens, 20, 22

D
debate, 16
democracy, 8, 20, 22

E
effectiveness, 16

F
fighting, 6, 18

G
government, 8, 10, 16, 18
greater good, 20

L
laws, 10
leaders, 18

P
point of view, 8, 12
principles, 18

V
values, 16, 22

WEBSITES

Due to the changing nature of Internet links, PowerKids Press has developed an online list of websites related to the subject of this book. This site is updated regularly. Please use this link to access the list: www.powerkidslinks.com/pofd/comp